A POCKET GUIDE TO . . .

Logic & Faith

Discerning truth

by Dr. Jason Lisle

THE FALLACY OF REIFICATION • THE FALLACY OF EQUIVOCATION • THE FALLACY OF
BEGGING THE QUESTION • THE COMPLEX QUESTION • BIFURCATION • FAULTY APPEAL TO
AUTHORITY • AD HOMINEM • THE STRAWMAN FALLACY • FORMAL FALLACIES • ATHEISM:
AN IRRATIONAL WORLDVIEW • GOD & NATURAL LAW • FAITH VS. REASON

A POCKET GUIDE TO . . .

Logic & Faith

Discerning truth in logical arguments

Dr. Jason Lisle

Petersburg, Kentucky, USA

Reprinted May 2016

ISBN: 978-1-60092-423-1

Printed in China

AnswersInGenesis.org

Table of Contents

Introduction

Whenever I hear people debating some issue (abortion, gun control, origins, religion, politics, etc.), I often spot a number of mistakes in their arguments. Mistakes in reasoning are called "logical fallacies," and they abound in origins debates. I have often thought it would be fun to carry a little buzzer that I could push when someone makes a fundamental mistake in reasoning. Of course, that would be impolite. However, we should all become familiar with logical fallacies so that our mental buzzer goes off whenever we hear a mistake in reasoning.

Logic (the study of correct and incorrect reasoning) has become a lost skill in our culture. And that is a shame. It is a very valuable tool, particularly for the Christian who wants to defend his or her faith better. Evolutionists often commit logical fallacies, and it is important that creationists learn to identify and refute such faulty reasoning. Sadly, I often see creationists committing logical fallacies as well. There is hardly anything more embarrassing than someone who advocates your position, but does so using bad reasoning!

Logic involves the use of arguments. When some people think of "arguments," they think of an emotionally heated exchange—a "yelling match." But that is not what is meant here. An argument is a chain of statements (called "propositions") in which the truth of one is asserted on the basis of the other(s). Biblically, we are supposed to argue in this way; we are to provide a reasoned defense (an argument) for the Christian faith (1 Peter 3:15) with gentleness and respect. An argument takes certain information as accepted (this is called a "premise"), and then proceeds to demonstrate that another claim must also be true (called the "conclusion"). Here is an example:

"Dr. Lisle is not in the office today. So, he is probably working at home."

In this argument, the first sentence is the premise: "Dr. Lisle is not in the office today." The arguer has assumed that we all agree to this premise and then draws the conclusion that "he is probably working at home." This is a reasonable argument; the conclusion does seem likely given the premise. So, this is called a "cogent" argument. This type of argument is classified as an *inductive* argument because the conclusion is likely, but not proved, from the premise. (After all, Dr. Lisle could be on vacation.) If the conclusion were *not* very likely given the premise, then the argument would be considered "weak" rather than "cogent."

The other type of argument is called a *deductive* argument. With this type of argument, it is asserted that the conclusion *definitely* follows from the premises (not just *probably*). For example:

"All dogs are mammals. And all mammals have hair. Therefore, all dogs have hair."

The conclusion of this argument definitely follows from the premises. That is, if the premises are true, then the conclusion has to be true as well. So, this is a *valid* argument. If the conclusion did not follow for a deductive argument, then the argument would be *invalid*.

In this pocket guide, we will explore the most common logical fallacies. It is very helpful to know these fallacies so that we can spot them when evolutionists commit them—and so that we do not commit them as well. In the Christian worldview, to be logical is to think in a way that is consistent with God's thinking. God is logical.

As Christians, we have a moral obligation to think and act rationally—to line up our thinking with God's truth (Ephesians

5:1; Isaiah 55:7–8). We pray that this pocket guide will be God-honoring, and will tremendously improve your defense of the faith.

Darwin used the Galápagos' finches to demonstrate "natural selection." But nature cannot select anything.

The Fallacy of Reification

Reification is attributing a concrete characteristic to something that is abstract. Perhaps you have heard the old saying, "It's not nice to fool Mother Nature." This is an example of reification because "nature" is an abstraction; it is simply the name we give to the chain of events in the universe. Nature is not a person and cannot literally be fooled, since nature does not have a mind. So, this expression would not make sense if taken literally.

Of course, not all language should be taken literally. There is nothing wrong with reification as a figure of speech. It is perfectly acceptable in poetry. Even the Bible uses reification at times in its poetic sections. For example, *Proverbs 8* personifies the concept of wisdom. This is a perfectly acceptable (and poetically beautiful) use of reification.

However, when reification is used as part of a *logical argument,* it is a fallacy. The reason for this is that using such a poetic expression is often ambiguous and can obscure important points in a debate. It is very common for evolutionists to commit this fallacy. Let's look at some examples of the *fallacy of*

THIS EVIDENCE SAYS EVOLUTION IS TRUE!

I SAID NO SUCH THING!

reification as they are commonly used in evolutionary arguments.

Sometimes in an argument, an evolutionist will say something like this: "*Nature* has designed some amazing creatures." This sentence commits the fallacy of reification because nature does not have a mind and cannot literally design anything. By using the fallacy of reification, the evolutionist obscures the fact that the evolution worldview really cannot account for the design of living creatures. (Keep in mind that he may be doing this unintentionally). God can design creatures because God is a person. Nature is a concept and cannot design anything.

"Creationists say the world was created supernaturally, but *science* says otherwise." Here the person has attributed personal, concrete attributes to the concept of *science.* In doing so, he or she overlooks the important fact that the *scientists* draw conclusions about the evidence and verbalize such conclusions—not "science." Science is a conceptual tool that can be used properly or improperly. It says nothing. It does not take a position on issues. So, this common example of reification is logically fallacious.

"The *evidence* speaks for itself." This expression is quite common, but when used as part of an argument, it is the fallacy of reification. Evidence does not speak at all. Evidence is a concept: the name we give to a body of facts that we believe to be consistent with a particular point of view. People draw conclusions about evidence and verbalize their thoughts. But evidence itself does not have thoughts to verbalize.

"*Evolution* figured out a way around these problems." I have a heard a number of evolutionists say something along these lines when attempting to explain some intricately designed biological system. But, of course, evolution is a concept. It has no mind and cannot figure out anything. So, this example again obscures the difficulty in accounting for design in the universe without appealing to a mind. It is a fallacious use of reification.

Even the phrase *natural selection* is an example of reification and could be considered a fallacy if used in an argument. Nature cannot literally select. This phrase is so commonly used that we might not call it a fallacy providing the meaning is understood by all. We do believe in the concept called "natural selection." Yes, organisms that are well-suited to an environment are more likely to survive than those that are not well-suited. (This is tautologically true and is something that both creationists and evolutionists believe).

But, suppose we asked, "Why is it that animals are well-suited to their environment?" If an evolutionist answered "natural selection," this would be the fallacy of reification. It poetically obscures the true reason that animals are designed to survive—God.

If you think about it, natural selection does not actually explain why we find organisms suited to their environment. It only explains why we do *not* find organisms that are *unsuited* to their environment (i.e., because they die). It is God—not "nature"—who has given living beings the abilities they need to survive.

Just like the old shell game, evolutionists use sleight of hand to change the meaning of the word *evolution* in mid-sentence.

The Fallacy of Equivocation

When debating on any topic, it is very important that we pay close attention to the meaning of words and how they are being used in the debate. Most words have more than one meaning, but only one of these meanings will properly fit the given context. When someone shifts from one meaning of a word to another within an argument, he or she has committed the fallacy of equivocation.

Here is a facetious example: "Doctors know a lot about medicine, and Dr. Lisle is a doctor. So, he must know a lot about medicine." This short argument shifts from one meaning of the word *doctor* (medical doctor) to another (PhD), making the argument fallacious. This use of equivocation is sometimes called a "bait and switch" fallacy because the listener is baited on one meaning of a word, and then the meaning is switched to draw a faulty conclusion.

Evolutionists often commit the fallacy of equivocation on the word *evolution*. This word has a number of meanings. *Evolution* can mean "change" in a general sense, but it can also refer to the idea that organisms share a common ancestor. Either meaning is perfectly legitimate, but the two meanings should not be conflated within an argument. Many evolutionists seem to think that by demonstrating evolution in the sense of "change," that it proves evolution in the sense of "common descent."

You might hear them say something like, "Creationists are wrong because we can see evolution happening all the time. Organisms are constantly changing and adapting to their environment." But, of course, the fact that animals change does not demonstrate that they share a common ancestor.

I cannot overstate how common this fallacy is in evolutionary arguments. Bacteria becoming resistant to antibiotics, speciation events, changes in the size and shape of finch beaks, the development of new breeds of dog, and changes in allele frequency are all examples of *change,* but none of them demonstrate that the basic kinds of organisms share a common ancestor. When you hear evolutionists cite these as examples of "evolution in action," you need to politely point out that they have committed the fallacy of equivocation.

You might notice that at Answers in Genesis, we often use phrases like "particles-to-people evolution." This may seem overly cumbersome, but we do this precisely to avoid equivocation.

Another word on which people sometimes equivocate is the word *science. Science* commonly refers to the procedures by which we explore the consistent and predictable behavior of the universe today—the scientific method. This is operational science. But *science* can also refer to a body of knowledge (e.g., the science of genetics). Furthermore, *science* can also refer to models regarding past events; this is origins science. Or it can refer to a specific model. When any of these meanings are switched within an argument, it is an instance of the fallacy of equivocation.

"Science has given us computers, medicine, the space program, and so much more. Why then do you deny the science of evolution?" This argument conflates operational science with one particular model of origins science. Origins science lacks the testable/repeatable aspects of operational science because the past can never be tested directly, nor repeated. Computers, medicine, and so on are all an outworking of operational science (the study of how the universe operates today).

By conflating operational science with evolution, the arguer hopes to give evolution a credibility that it does not truly deserve. Yes, we do believe in operational science, and we have some respect for origins science as well. However, this does not mean that we should believe in evolution—which is only one particular model of origins science.

Old-earth creationists often commit this fallacy on the word *interpretation*. They may say, "We must always compare our interpretation of Scripture with our interpretation of nature." Interpretation of the Scripture means to understand the meaning of the propositional statements—to grasp the author's intention. However, nature does not have intentions. When we interpret nature, we are *creating* propositional statements about nature. This is very different than understanding propositional statements that someone else has already created. By conflating these two meanings of *interpretation,* the old-earth creationist places scientist's statements about nature on the same level as Scripture.

The SETI program is based on the fallacy of begging the question since researchers assume that humans evolved on earth and therefore other intelligent life must have evolved somewhere in the universe.

The Fallacy of Begging the Question

I once did a telescope session with a small group of people, including a four-year-old boy who was particularly interested in astronomy. I asked this young budding astronomer if he believed in alien spaceships. "Of course," he said. I then asked him why he believed in alien spaceships. I'll never forget his clever response: "How else would the aliens get here?" Pretty logical isn't it? The aliens would never be able to get to earth without a spaceship. So, clearly, there must be alien spaceships!

This is a wonderful example of a very common error in reasoning—the fallacy of begging the question. This fallacy is committed when a person merely assumes what he or she is attempting to prove or when the premise of an argument actually depends upon its conclusion. In this case, our young student was attempting to prove the existence of alien spacecraft by taking it for granted that aliens have traveled to earth. But that is essentially the point in question. This young aspiring astronomer was reasoning in a circle.

Of course, we expect such humorous reasoning from a four-year-old. As we grow up, we are expected to become rational and not make these kinds of logical mistakes. That's why it is so disturbing to find that many adults commit the fallacy of begging the question in debates on origins. Some examples are obvious: "Evolution must be true because it is a fact." But, more commonly, the fallacy is much more subtle. Consider some of the following arguments.

"The Bible cannot be true because it contains miracles. And miracles would violate the laws of nature!"

Yes, miracles can potentially involve a temporary suspension of the laws of nature (not that all of them necessarily do).[1] Since the Bible makes it clear that God is beyond natural laws, He can suspend/violate them if He wishes to. But the critic's argument has simply taken it for granted that violations of the laws of nature are impossible. In other words, the arguer has already assumed that the Bible is false—in order to argue that the Bible is false. He has begged the question.

You may have heard people argue:

> "The Bible cannot be true because it teaches that the earth is only thousands of years old; whereas, we know the earth is billions of years old."

All such arguments commit the fallacy of begging the question. Here is why. Old earth arguments are all based on the assumptions of naturalism (nature is all that there is) and a large degree of uniformitarianism (present rates and processes are representative of past rates and processes). Then, by extrapolating from present rates of various earth processes, the person estimates how long it would take to build up or erode certain geological features or how long it would take for a radioisotope to decay.

But the Bible denies naturalism and uniformitarianism (e.g., erosion rates during the global flood). By assuming naturalism and uniformitarianism, the critic has already merely assumed that the Bible is wrong. He then uses this assumption to conclude that the Bible is wrong. His reasoning is circular.

> "Creation cannot be true because you would have to ignore all that scientific evidence."

But this argument begs the question because it presupposes that scientific evidence somehow provides support for evolution, which has not been demonstrated.

> "It makes no sense to deny evolution; it is a well-established fact of nature."

This argument also begs the question since the truth status of evolution is the very question at issue.

Christians are not always above circular reasoning either. Some have argued,

> "The Bible must be the Word of God because it says it is. And what it says must be true, since God cannot lie."

Of course, it is quite true that the Bible does claim to be the Word of God, and it is also true that God does not lie. But when one of these statements is used as the sole support for the other, the argument commits the fallacy of begging the question. The same line of argumentation could be used to "prove" the Koran, which of course we would deny.

Now, it's time to get a little philosophically deep. Brace yourself. Begging the question is a very strange fallacy because it is actually *valid*. Recall that a valid argument is one in which the conclusion does follow from the premises. Normally fallacies are not valid; the fact that their conclusion does not follow from the premise(s) is what makes them fallacies. But, oddly, with begging the question the conclusion does follow from the premise (because it is simply a restatement of the premise). So, the argument, "Evolution must be true because it is a fact," is valid. But if it is valid, then why is it considered a fallacy?

The answer would seem to be that begging the question is a fallacy because it is *arbitrary*. Circular arguments of this kind are not useful because anyone who denies the conclusion would also deny the premise (since the conclusion is essentially the same as the premise). So, the argument, "Evolution must be true because it is a fact," while technically valid, is fallacious because the arguer has merely assumed what he is trying to prove. Arbitrary assumptions are not to be used in logical reasoning because we could equally well assume the exact opposite. It would be just as legitimate to argue, "Evolution cannot be true because it is false."

It should also be noted that there are certain special cases where circular reasoning is unavoidable and not necessarily fallacious. Remember that begging the question is not invalid; it is considered fallacious because it is arbitrary. But what if it were not arbitrary? There are some situations where the conclusion of an argument must be assumed at the outset, but is not arbitrary.[2] Here is an example:

1. Without laws of logic, we could not make an argument.

2. We can make an argument.

3. Therefore, there must be laws of logic.

This argument is perfectly reasonable, and valid. But it is subtly circular. This argument is using a law of logic called *modus tollens* to prove that there are laws of logic. So, we have tacitly assumed what we are trying to prove. But it is absolutely unavoidable in this case. We must use laws of logic to prove anything—even the existence of laws of logic.

However, the above argument is not arbitrary. We do have a good reason for assuming laws of logic, since without them we couldn't prove anything. And perhaps most significantly, anyone attempting to disprove the existence of laws of logic would have to first assume that laws of logic do exist in order to make the argument. He would refute himself.

Most of the examples of circular reasoning used by evolutionists are of the fallacious begging-the-question variety—they are arbitrary. Consider the evolutionist who argues:

"The Bible cannot be correct because it says that stars were created in a single day; but we now know that it takes millions of years for stars to form."

By assuming that stars form over millions of years, the critic has taken for granted that they were not supernaturally created. He has tacitly assumed the Bible is wrong in his attempt to argue that the Bible is wrong; he has begged the question. Another example is:

"We know evolution must have happened, because we are here!"

This argument begs the question, since the way we got here is the very point in question.

Watch for arguments that subtly presume (in an arbitrary way) what the critic is attempting to prove. In particular, evolutionists will often take for granted the assumptions of naturalism, uniformitarianism, strict empiricism (the notion that all truth claims are answered by observation and experimentation), and sometimes evolution itself. But, of course, these are the very claims at issue. When an evolutionist takes these things for granted, he is not giving a good logical reason for his position; he is simply arbitrarily asserting his position.

---

1. The parting of the Red Sea was certainly a miracle—an extraordinary act of God (Exodus 14:21). Yet, God used wind—a force of nature—to accomplish this miracle.

2. It is always necessary to presuppose the preconditions of intelligibility. These include laws of logic and induction. However, the evolutionist assumes these arbitrarily—without rational justification—and has thus begged the question. The Christian can account for logic and induction within his worldview.

Reporters sometimes use emotional language which shows their bias rather than just stating the "facts."

The Fallacy of the Question-Begging Epithet

One of the most common fallacies committed by evolutionists on the Internet is the fallacy of the question-begging epithet. This could be considered a specific sub-type of begging the question (the fallacy of merely assuming what one is trying to prove).

With the question-begging epithet, the arguer uses biased (often emotional) language to persuade people rather than using logic. For example, if a reporter said,

> "This criminal is charged with violently murdering the innocent victim,"

she would be using a question-begging epithet because she has used biased language to make a case that is not yet logically established. It would have been more objective for her to say,

> "This suspect is charged with killing the other person."

Some great examples of question-begging epithets can be found on some evolution internet sites—particularly forums or blogs. I saw one example where an evolutionist wrote,

> "Our department is becoming infested with creationists."

The word *infested* is emotionally charged and portrays creationists in a bad light without making any argument for this. Another writer stated,

> "To be a creationist, you'd have to ignore tons of scientific evidence."

This remark is the fallacy of the question-begging epithet because it uses biased language (and not logic) to suggest that scientific evidence supports evolution.

There is a place for emotional language. After all, language has other purposes than to make logical arguments. It can be used to inform, to question, to command, and to evoke. However, when people try to evoke an emotional response to persuade others of a point that is logically questionable, the fallacy of the question-begging epithet is committed.

Yelling or vulgar language during a debate is always an example of this fallacy. Many times people will turn up the vocal volume to compensate for a lack of cogency in their argument. Ironically, many of those who use mocking or vulgar language in forums seem to think that their rhetoric constitutes a good argument. Far from it. Such language is an indication of a serious lack of critical thinking skills.[1]

Question-begging epithets can be subtle. Consider this phrase: "evolution vs. creationism." By attaching -*ism* to the end of creation but not to evolution, the

person is subtly suggesting that creation is merely a belief, whereas evolution is not. But he or she has made no argument for this.

"Creationists believe that the universe is young, but the best scientists tell us that it is billions of years old."

By using the adjective to describe those scientists who believe in an old universe, this argument uses biased language rather than logic to persuade. It is fallacious.

Here is another example:

"The Creation 'Museum' isn't about science at all, but is entirely about a peculiar, quirky, very specific interpretation of the Bible."

The author provided no support for this opinion; it is simply an emotional reaction. He also attempts to deride the Creation Museum by putting the word *museum* in quotes. His claim is nothing but a fallacious epithet. When people use sarcastic/sardonic statements in place of logic, they commit the fallacy of the question-begging epithet. For example,

"Yeah Tyrannosauridae were herbovirus [sic] too before The Fall [sic]. With razor sharp teeth to kill the tenacious shrubberies!"

Such statements are designed to stir people's emotions, thereby distracting them from the realization that no logical case has been made.

Another common example is when someone accuses an opponent of committing a logical fallacy when it is not the case. A false accusation of a logical fallacy is itself a logical fallacy. This might happen, for example, after a creationist has politely and cogently pointed out a number of fallacies in an evolutionist's reasoning, and then makes a good argument for creation. In an attempt to turn the tables, the evolutionist responds by saying,

"Well, that's a fallacy!"

But he has made no logical case that the creationist has indeed committed a fallacy, which makes the evolutionist's claim itself an arbitrary question-begging epithet.

In Ephesians 5:6 we read, "Let no one deceive you with empty words, for because of these things the wrath of God comes upon the sons of disobedience." An evolutionist may be very emotionally committed to his position and may use biased (or mocking) language in an attempt to evoke a similar emotion in others. However, this is logically irrelevant to whether or not his belief is true.

When people use mere rhetoric ("empty words") without providing a logical reason for their position, we must cordially point out that they have not made a logical argument; they are simply being arbitrary. Conversely, Christians are to take the "high ground" and always give a good reason for the confidence within us (1 Peter 3:15).

---

1.   There are several evolution blogs that consist of virtually nothing but emotionally charged language. The authors make no logical case for their position, and students of logic will easily recognize that such rhetoric is nothing more than emotional venting (much like a child throwing a tantrum).

Trial lawyers can be quite good at asking loaded or leading questions to confuse a witness.

The Complex Question

Similar to the question-begging epithet is the fallacy called *complex question*. This is the interrogative form of begging the question—when the arguer attempts to persuade by asking a loaded question. A classic example is this: "Have you stopped beating your wife?" Either a yes or no answer would seem to imply that the person did in the past beat his wife, which may not be the case. The question is "complex" because it should be divided into two questions:

1. Did you ever beat your wife?

2. If so, have you now stopped doing this?

Here are some common evolutionary examples of the fallacy of complex question:

"Why are creationists against science?"

This loaded question presumes that creationists are against science, which is not the case. It should have been divided:

1. Are creationists against science?

2. If so, why?

Since the answer to the first is no, the second question is not necessary.

"Why is evolution so critical to our understanding of biology?" is fallacious because we should first ask, "Is evolution critical to our understanding of biology?"

Watch for leading questions in evolutionary literature such as, "How were dinosaurs able to survive for millions of years?" This is the fallacy of the complex question because it should be divided:

1. Did dinosaurs indeed survive for millions of years?

2. If so, how?

   • "What is the mechanism by which reptiles evolved into birds?"

   • "If the earth truly is 6000 years old as you creationists say, then why do we find rocks that are over 4 billion years old?"

   • "If creation is true, then why does all the scientific evidence point to evolution?"

These all are fallacious questions which used biased language to persuade rather than logic.

One time, after I gave a presentation on creation, an atheist came up to me and asked, "Are you aware of the fact that . . . ?" Before he could complete the sentence, I strongly suspected that it was going to be the fallacy of the complex question. Sure enough, what he was rhetorically asserting to be a fact was not true at all. He had misunderstood some of the things I had presented and had committed some errors in reasoning as well. People sometimes use the formula "Are you aware of the fact that X?" to persuade others of X, when in fact X is logically unproved.

What people judge to be a fallacy often depends on their worldview. Consider this question:

"Have you repented of your sins?"

A non-Christian may consider this to be a complex question and would want it divided:

1. Have you ever sinned?

2. If so, have you repented?

From a Christian worldview, however, the question is not complex because we know that all have sinned (Romans 3:23).

Along with the question-begging epithet, the complex question uses biased language in place of logical argumentation. When the evolutionists commit either of these fallacies, we must gently point out that they have not actually made a logical argument. They have rhetorically assumed what they are trying to prove and have, thus, begged the very question at issue.

Bifurcation

A person commits the fallacy of bifurcation when he or she claims that there are only two mutually exclusive possibilities—when, in fact, there is a third option. For this reason the fallacy is also known as the *either-or fallacy* and the *false dilemma*.

A facetious example is this:

"Either the traffic light is red, or it is green."

This is obviously fallacious, since the light could be yellow.[1]

A more realistic example is this:

"Either you have faith or you are rational."

This commits the fallacy of bifurcation, since there is a third possibility: we can have faith *and* be rational. In fact, faith is essential in order to have rationality (e.g., to make sense of laws of logic).[2]

"Either the universe operates in a law-like fashion, or God is constantly performing miracles."

This is also fallacious because a third possibility exists: the universe operates in a law-like fashion most of the time, and God occasionally performs a miracle.

Sometimes the origins debate is framed as "faith vs. reason," "science or religion," or the "Bible vs. science." These are all false dilemmas. Faith and reason are not contrary. They go well together (since all reasoning presupposes a type of faith).[3]

Likewise, science and religion (the Christian religion to be specific) are not mutually exclusive. In fact, it is the Christian system that makes sense of science and the uniformity of nature. Likewise the debate should never be framed as "the Bible vs. science," since the procedures of science are fully compatible with the Bible. In fact, science is based on the biblical worldview; science requires predictability in nature, which is only made possible by the fact that God upholds the universe in a consistent way that is congenial to human understanding. Such predictability just wouldn't make sense in a "chance" universe.

The fallacy of bifurcation may be more difficult to spot when the person merely implies that only two options exist, rather than explicitly stating this.

"I could never live by faith because I am a rational person."

This sentence tacitly presents us with only two options: either faith, or rationality. But, as we've mentioned before, these are not exclusive. A rational person must have some degree of faith. So, the Christian takes the third, unmentioned option: faith *and* rationality.[4]

"The Bible teaches that 'in Christ all things hold together.' But we now know that the forces of gravity and electromagnetism are what hold the universe together."

This is an example of the fallacy of bifurcation because the critic has implicitly assumed that either (1) God holds the universe together, or (2) gravity and electromagnetism do. However, these are not exclusive. "Gravity" and "electromagnetism" are simply the names we give to the way in which God holds the universe together. Laws of nature are not a replacement for God's power. Rather, they are an *example* of God's power.[5]

"You must not really believe that God is going to answer your request for healing; otherwise you would not have gone to the doctor."

The implicit false dilemma here is that either the doctor will help the person or God will. But why can't it be both? God can use human actions as part of the means by which He accomplishes His will.

On the other hand, in some situations there really are only two options; and it is not fallacious to say so. "Either my car is in the garage, or it is not the case that my car is in the garage" commits no fallacy.[6] When Jesus states, "He who is not with Me is against Me" (Matthew 12:30, NAS), He has not committed any fallacy because God is in a position to tell us that there is no third ("neutral") option. (An attempt to be neutral toward God is sinful and, therefore, non-neutral.)[7] The key to spotting fallacies of bifurcation is to watch for cases when only two options are presented (either explicitly or implicitly) and to consider carefully whether or not there is a third possibility.

---

1. In logic, red and green are said to be contrary, but not contradictory options. When two propositions are contradictory, one of them is true, and the other is false. A proposition can be turned into its contradiction by adding "It is not the case that." So, the statements "The light is red" and "It is not the case that the light is red" are contradictory. However, when two propositions are contrary, they can both be false, but they cannot both be true.

2. For the demonstration of this, see Jason Lisle, *The Ultimate Proof of Creation* (Master Books, 2009).

3. Faith is belief in what has not been observed by the senses (see Hebrews 11:1). In order to reason logically, a person must believe in laws of logic. However, laws of logic are immaterial and therefore cannot be observed by the senses. So, belief in laws of logic is a type of faith. Moreover, laws of logic only have rational justification in the Christian faith system.

4. To be specific, it is "rationality *because* of faith." It is the Christian faith that makes rationality possible.

5. Otherwise, there would be no reason to think that the laws of nature apply universally or that they will apply in the future as they have in the past. Only the consistent Christian has rational justification for such uniformity in nature.

6. There can be no third option when the two options are X and not-X. This is the law of the excluded middle.

7. Our thinking is to be in submission to Christ (2 Corinthians 10:5). When the critic attempts to be "neutral," he is refusing to submit his thinking to Christ. The critic's position is rebellious and, therefore, non-neutral.

Ad Hominem

The phrase *ad hominem* is Latin and means "to the man." The fallacy is so named because it directs an argument against the *person* making a claim rather than the claim itself. The critic hopes that people will believe the claim in question is false simply on the basis that there is something objectionable about the person making the claim. For example, "You cannot honestly accept John's claims about politics because he can't even find a job!" However, John's inability to find employment is logically irrelevant to the political claim he is making.

The fallacy comes in two varieties: abusive *ad hominem* and circumstantial *ad hominem*. In the abusive *ad hominem,* the critic attacks his opponent's character or insults him in an attempt to discredit him in the eyes of the audience. This tactic is common in politics, and it may psychologically sway people. However, it is *logically* fallacious because a person's character (or lack thereof) is logically irrelevant to the validity of his argument. Even if the critic's negative claims about his opponent are true (e.g., he really is a draft-dodger, or he really did spend time in jail), this has no bearing on the position he is advocating.

Name-calling is perhaps the most obvious form of the abusive *ad hominem* fallacy. When children have a heated disagreement, they sometimes engage in such behavior. As we grow up, we are supposed to become rational and learn to make arguments based on logical reasoning. However, since there is no rationally sound argument for evolution, evolutionists are increasingly resorting to name-calling. I recall a particular instance where an evolutionist launched into a name-calling diatribe against Ken

Ham.[1] Such immature behavior reminds us that the evolutionary worldview is utterly intellectually bankrupt.[2]

The circumstantial *ad hominem* fallacy is when a critic simply dismisses a person's argument based on the arguer's circumstances. Suppose Susie makes an argument that taxes on gasoline should be increased. Her opponent, Bobby, tries to refute this by pointing out that Susie's job is tax-supported, so she is strongly motivated to argue for higher taxes. Bobby concludes that Susie's argument is wrong since Susie has a bias. Bobby has committed the circumstantial *ad hominem* fallacy—just because Susie is strongly motivated to defend a particular position does not mean that her argument is faulty.

A non-Christian might argue:

"Christianity isn't true. You just believe in Christianity because you were brought up in a Christian home. If you were brought up in the Islam religion, you would be a Muslim now."

This is the circumstantial *ad hominem* fallacy because the circumstances by which the person became a Christian are not relevant to his or her argument for Christianity. While it may be true that I am much more likely to become a Christian by virtue of being reared in a Christian home, this is utterly irrelevant to whether or not I have a really good logical argument for Christianity. It would be just like saying, "You just believe in the multiplication table because you were taught it in school!" It is true that I probably would not have discovered the multiplication table without someone teaching it to me, but this does not mean that I don't have some really good reasons to continue to believe in the multiplication table!

An evolutionist might argue:

"Creation isn't true. You just believe in creation because you read that stuff on the Answers in Genesis website!"

Although the information on the website may have helped people to see the truth of creation and how to argue for it (we hope so!), the person's argument should be evaluated on its own merit, not on how he arrived at it. The evolutionist is wrong to simply dismiss an argument because he doesn't like the source.[3] The source is not relevant to the argument's validity.

It may help to note that there is often a difference between a *cause* and a *reason*. What is the *cause* of a person believing in the Christian worldview? Many factors may have contributed: conversations with family, a sermon, prayers of friends, and ultimately the Holy Spirit.[4]

What is the *reason* (i.e., the rational justification) for a person believing in the Christian worldview? One really good reason would be that Christianity alone can account laws of logic,[5] and science.[6] In the above examples, the critic is arbitrarily dismissing a *reason* for a position on the basis that he does not like the *cause* of the person coming to that position. But such a dismissal is logically unwarranted and fallacious.

Not all references to a person's character are necessarily *ad hominem* fallacies. For example, if a person makes a particular assertion (not an argument, but merely an assertion), and if it can be demonstrated that the person is generally dishonest, it would be perfectly appropriate and relevant to point out that his dishonesty calls into question his credibility on the claim.[7] However, even this does not *disprove* the person's assertion, since a generally dishonest person will sometimes tell the truth. Moreover, if the person makes an *argument,* his or her alleged dishonesty is totally irrelevant to the validity of that argument. (An argument is not the same as an assertion.)[8] The key is to remember that an argument should be based on its merit, not on the alleged character defects or the circumstances of the person making the argument.

1. See "Evolving Tactics" (http://www.answersingenesis.org/articles/am/v4/n1/evolving-tactics).

2. Evolution cannot account for rationality, morality, or the success of science, as documented in my book *The Ultimate Proof of Creation*.

3. Phrased this way, such a mistake in reasoning is called the *genetic fallacy*.

4. 1 Corinthians 12:3.

5. See "Atheism: An Irrational Worldview," page 65.

6. See "Evolution: The Anti-science" (http://www.answersingenesis.org/articles/aid/v3/n1/evolution-anti-science).

7. However, people cannot rationally assert that their opponent is lying on the basis that they disagree on the very claim at issue—that would be begging the question. As an example, consider the evolutionist who says, "Creationists are liars because they teach that the universe is only thousands of years old and that the first life on earth was supernaturally created." The evolutionist's assertion is only true if evolution is, but that is the very claim at issue. So, the evolutionist has simply begged the question.

8. An assertion is a proposition, whereas an argument is a chain of propositions where the truth of one is claimed to follow from the others. Logical fallacies concern the "chain of reasoning" between propositions, not the truthfulness of the propositions themselves. See Introduction, page 7.

Images of scientists in white lab coats are often used in ads and commercials because they lend an air of authority.

Faulty Appeal to Authority

The faulty appeal to authority is, in a way, the opposite of the *ad hominem* fallacy. Whereas the *ad hominem* fallacy denies a claim based on the person making it, the faulty appeal to authority endorses a claim simply based on the person making it. Essentially, the faulty appeal to authority is the argument that a claim is true simply because someone else believes it.

The basic structure of the argument is this:

1. Bill believes X.

2. Therefore, X is true.

Of course, it is almost never stated this explicitly. Often, the person to whom the appeal is made is considered highly esteemed for one reason or another. But the truthfulness of the claim at issue is not necessarily relevant to the popularity of the individual making the claim.

In the origins debate, the faulty appeal is often to someone who is considered an expert on a particular topic—a scientist or perhaps a theologian. For example, "Dr. Bill has a PhD in biology, and he believes in evolution." The unstated conclusion is that evolution must therefore be true or is at least likely to be true. But such an argument is fallacious. After all, we could equally point out that "Dr. Dave also has a PhD in biology, and he believes in *biblical creation*." The fact that other experts on the topic draw the opposite conclusion should reveal the vacuous nature of the evolutionist's argument.

Another example would be this:

"Jim has a doctorate in theology, and he says it's okay to believe in evolution and the Bible."

Again, we could certainly find many qualified theologians who would state the exact opposite. While it is okay to consider what a theologian has to say about the Bible, it is infinitely more important to consider what the Bible actually states!

If an expert on U.S. law claimed that the Constitution does not contain the phrase "We the people," would that make it so? We could easily refute his claim by simply reading from an actual copy of the Constitution. The fact that he is an expert does not override the evidence.

Not all appeals to authority are *faulty* appeals to authority. It is legitimate to consider the opinion of an expert on a particular topic. None of us has the time or the ability to verify each and every truth claim that has ever been made. We can and should rely upon the expertise of others at times. So, when does the appeal to authority become a fallacy? It seems there are three common ways in which this occurs:

1. **Appealing to an expert in an area that is not his area of expertise.** Our hypothetical Dr. Bill may indeed have a PhD in biology—and that qualifies him to say something about how organisms function today. But does knowledge of how things work today necessarily imply knowledge of how things came to be? This is a separate question. The experiments Dr. Bill has done and the observations he has made have all taken place in the present world. He has no more direct observations of the ancient past than anyone else today.[1] The question of origins is a history question that deals with worldviews. It is not really a biology question, and, so, Dr. Bill's opinion on the topic of origins isn't necessarily any more qualified than any other opinion.

2. **Failure to consider the worldview of the expert and how this might affect his interpretation of the data.** We all have a world-and-life view—a philosophy that guides our understanding of the universe. When we interpret scientific and historical evidence, we use this philosophy to draw conclusions.[2] The fact that Dr. Bill believes in evolution means that he is predisposed to interpret the evidence in a particular way. (My point is not to fault him for this; everyone has biases. Rather, we should simply be mindful of what his biases are). A creationist with the same credentials might draw a very different conclusion from the same data. So, while I may put confidence in what Dr. Bill says about the structure of a particular protein that he has studied under the microscope, his bias against biblical creation means it would be unwise for me to trust his opinions on questions of origins.

3. **Treating a fallible expert as infallible.** We should also keep in mind that even experts do not know everything. They can make mistakes even in their own field. Some new discovery may cause a scientist to change his mind about something that he thought he knew. So, at best, appealing to an expert yields only a probable conclusion. It would be fallacious to argue that something definitely must be true simply because a (fallible) expert believes it.

Of course, if the expert had knowledge of everything and never lied, then there would be no fallacy in accepting his statements as absolutely true. In fact, it would be absurd to not do so under those circumstances. The Bible claims to be such an infallible source—a revelation from the God who knows everything and cannot lie.[3] Thus, there is no fallacy in appealing to Scripture as absolutely authoritative. Some evolutionists have mistakenly accused creationists of committing the faulty appeal to authority on this very issue.

Another type of faulty appeal to authority is the appeal to the majority. This is when a person argues that a claim must be true simply because most people believe it. But, of course, just because a majority of people believe something does not make it so. History is replete with examples of when the majority was totally wrong. Truth is not decided by a vote, after all.

This fallacy is so obvious it is hard to believe that people would fall for it. But there is something very psychologically seductive about the appeal to the majority. We are inclined to think, "How could all those people be wrong?"[4] Of course, it could well be the case that many people in that majority are convinced of the claim at issue for exactly the same reason: because all the *other* people in that majority believe it (which is no *logical* reason at all.)

The appeal to the majority is often combined with the appeal to an expert—an appeal to the majority of experts. Evolutionists often commit this double-fallacy; they try to support their case by pointing out:

> "The vast majority of scientists believe in evolution. (Therefore, evolution is very likely to be true)."

However, simply adding two fallacies together does not form a good argument! Again, we could point to many historical examples of cases where the scientific consensus was dead wrong. Yet, people continue to perpetuate this fallacy.

We sometimes hear phrases like

> "According to mainstream science . . . ,"

> "The scientific establishment . . . ,"

> or

> "the scientific consensus is . . . ,"

as an alleged proof of a particular claim. Another example is this:

"Creationists teach that the world is roughly 6000 years old, but the majority of scientists disagree."

This sentence is true, but the unstated conclusion is that we must accept the opinion of the majority of experts—which is logically fallacious.

As with a single expert, it is not fallacious to consider the opinion of a group of experts. However, as before, we should consider whether they are qualified in the issue under investigation, be mindful of their worldview and biases, and keep in mind that they are fallible people with finite knowledge.

I believe that God gave people different interests and is pleased when they study hard and develop expertise on some aspect of His creation. It is commendable to esteem the opinion of experts, provided that we are discerning and never regard fallible human opinions above (or equal to) the authoritative Word of God.

---

1. For some reason, it is common for people to think that paleontologist and geologists study the past. But this is not so. Rocks and fossils exist in the present (otherwise we wouldn't have access to them). Although there is nothing wrong with speculating about past events (e.g., how fossils or rocks formed) and then testing the plausibility of such models with experiments in the present, we should keep in mind that the past is never actually observable or open to scientific investigation.

2. Some evolutionists might claim that they have no philosophy—that our interpretations of evidence should be "neutral" and unbiased. But this is a philosophy in and of itself, albeit a very bad one since it is self-refuting.

3. Colossians 2:3; Titus 1:2.

4. Sin is the answer to this question. All people have a sin nature. Those who have not had their minds regenerated by the Holy Spirit are not capable of drawing correct conclusions on spiritual matters (1 Corinthians 2:14). The unbeliever is not a neutral, objective observer. He is rebellious and strongly motivated to reject the biblical God (Romans 1:18–20).

Straw-Man Fallacy

*I*t's a fallacy that just shouldn't happen—but it does all the time. The straw-man fallacy is when a person misrepresents his opponent's position and then proceeds to refute that misrepresentation (i.e., the "straw man") rather than what his opponent actually claims.[1] Here's an example:

"Creationists do not believe that animals change. But clearly, animals do change. So, creationists are mistaken."

Since creationists do indeed believe that animals change (just not from one basic created kind to another), the argument is a straw-man fallacy. The argument does not refute what creationists *actually* claim.

Such a misrepresentation could be unintentional; it could be that a particular evolutionist simply misunderstands what a creationist is teaching. Or the fallacy could be quite deliberate. That, of course, is a dishonest approach, yet it is quite common in origins debates.

Even in cases where the misrepresentation is unintentional, there is still a degree of liability. After all, the arguer should have done sufficient research and studied what it is the opponent actually teaches. We would certainly be willing to overlook minor misunderstandings, particularly where a position is complex or nuanced (though the critic should still be corrected on the issue). However, there are a number of cases where the creationist position is so clear that misrepresentations by evolutionists are simply inexcusable. The following are a few examples.

If an evolutionist were to claim, "Creationists don't believe in science," this would be a straw-man fallacy.[2] Creationists do believe in science. There are several full-time PhD scientists on the Answers in Genesis staff. I've argued on the AiG website, as in my book (*The Ultimate Proof of Creation*) that biblical creation is what makes science possible.

Someone may claim, "Creationists believe in the fixity of species." However, this is certainly not the mainstream biblical creationist position. There may be a few individuals that hold to such a concept, but it is not the position advocated by most creationists. Thus, the generalization "creationists believe . . ." is false.

Likewise, the claim, "Creationists say there are no good mutations" is not representative of what biblical creationists teach. Generally, we say that mutations do not add brand-new, creative information to the genome and are thus in the "wrong direction" to make evolution happen. But we do believe that mutations can result in traits that increase survival value under certain conditions.

"Answers in Genesis is pushing to get creation to be taught in public schools alongside evolution."

This is definitely false. Answers in Genesis as a ministry is not about political or legal change. Rather, we are about defending the Bible from the very first verse and teaching other Christians to do the same. Although this may eventually result in a changed political and legal situation, we do not (as a ministry) attempt to change laws or get involved in politics.

> "The Bible teaches that the earth has literal pillars and corners and cannot be moved. It is clearly wrong."

This is a misrepresentation of Scripture and therefore constitutes a straw-man fallacy. The Bible uses figures of speech (just as we do when we say, "Tim is a pillar of the community") and poetic language at times. Referring to the cardinal directions as "corners"[3] or the stability of the earth as not able to "be moved"[4] is not an error. It is entirely inappropriate for a critic to take the poetic sections of the Bible as literal—or the literal historical sections as poetic. Many objections against Scripture turn out to be straw-man fallacies.

The claims that creationists believe in a flat earth, that we deny laws of nature, or that we take every verse of the Bible in a wooden literal sense are all baseless assertions. Nonetheless, claiming that creationists believe in such things makes the creation position easier to discredit—but it is not a rationally cogent way to debate. Granted, not all evolutionists do this; some do accurately represent their opponents. But ignorance of biblical creation among those who oppose it is a serious problem: one that Christian apologists must be prepared to face.

We must gently encourage our opponents to find out what it is that creationists actually teach. This is not a difficult task. Our positions on the most-asked questions are well-summarized in the *New Answers Book* series and to a great extent on the Answers in Genesis website (www.answersingenesis.org).

Creationists must also stay educated on both sides of the issue so that we do not commit the very same fallacy.[5] Watch for misrepresentations of creation or other Christian teachings and be ready to point out that such straw-man arguments are fallacious; yet always do so with gentleness and respect.

---

1. The straw-man fallacy is a specific type of the fallacy of irrelevant thesis. The latter is the fallacy of proving a point that is not at issue. In the case of the straw-man fallacy, proving that the misrepresentation of the opponent's position is false is irrelevant to whether or not his actual position is true or false.

2. It could also be an example of equivocation if the evolutionist conflates operational science with origins science or science with evolution.

3. Isaiah 11:12; the Hebrew word translated "corners" indicates an extremity, as in the farthest reaches of the earth. The four extremes would be north, south, east, and west. The Revelation 7:1 passage uses the same type of wording as Isaiah to indicate the same cardinal directions. Revelation often alludes to Old Testament imagery.

4. Psalm 93:1; the fact that this occurs in the Psalms is essentially a "giveaway" that it is a poetic passage. The Psalmist uses the same Hebrew word when he says, "I shall not be moved" (Psalm 62:6), indicating that he will not deviate from the path God created for him.

5. This doesn't seem to be quite as much of an issue, perhaps because our culture is so saturated with the notion of particles-to-people evolution. Evolution is taught in virtually all public schools in the United States (and usually biblical creation is not); so, most creationists are aware of the evolution position. We should also note that all Christians have at one point been non-Christians; so, we can understand how the unbeliever thinks about things. However, non-Christians have difficulty thinking like Christians (even if they were brought up in the church) because the crucial issues require the enlightening of the Holy Spirit. Indeed, the unbeliever cannot understand spiritual issues apart from God's power (1 Corinthians 2:14).

Formal Fallacies

The final logical fallacies we will address in this book are two of the most common fallacies that occur in arguments about origins: **affirming the consequent** and **denying the antecedent**. These are *formal* fallacies because the mistake in reasoning stems from the structure (the *form*) of the argument. It is well worth the effort to study formal fallacies and their corresponding terminology because these two fallacies are extremely common—perhaps the two most common fallacies committed by evolutionists.

Formal deductive arguments can be put into a symbolic notation with letters representing the propositions. Consider the proposition, "If it is snowing, then it must be cold outside." This proposition has the basic form: "If p, then q." Any proposition that has that form ("if p, then q") is called a "hypothetical proposition." This is because it's not asserting either p or q; it is merely stating that if p hypothetically were true, then q would have to be true as well. In a hypothetical proposition the first part (p) is called the antecedent, and the second part (q) is called the consequent. In our example, "it is snowing" is the antecedent, and "it must be cold outside" is the consequent.

If an argument has two premises, only one of which is hypothetical, then it is called a "mixed hypothetical syllogism." Here is an example:

1. If it is snowing, then it must be cold outside.

2. It is snowing.

3. Therefore, it is cold outside.

In this argument, the first premise (if p, then q) is hypothetical. The second premise (p) is not hypothetical; it asserts that it is indeed snowing. And the conclusion is q. Since the second premise affirms that p (the antecedent) is true, this type of argument is called "affirming the antecedent" and is perfectly valid. (Recall, "valid" means that if the premises are true, so is the conclusion). The Latin name for this type of argument is *modus ponens,* which means the "method of affirming."

Affirming the consequent

There is a fallacy that is very similar to *modus ponens* and has this form:

1. If p, then q.

2. q.

3. Therefore, p.

We can see that this is a fallacy by substituting phrases for p and q.

1. If it is snowing, then it must be cold outside.

2. It is cold outside.

3. Therefore, it must be snowing.

But clearly just because it is cold outside does not necessarily mean that it must be snowing. So, this argument is invalid. Since the second premise affirms that the consequent (q) is true, this fallacy is called "affirming the consequent." Here are some common examples:

1. If evolution were true, we would expect to see similarities in DNA of all organisms on earth.

2. We do see similarities in DNA of all organisms on earth.

3. Therefore, evolution is true.

The evolutionist making such an argument has failed to recognize that creationists would also expect to see similarities in

DNA of all organisms, since the original kinds were made by the same Creator.

1. If the big bang is true, then we would expect to see a cosmic microwave background.

2. We do see a cosmic microwave background.

3. Therefore, the big bang must be true.

This big bang supporter has failed to consider other possible causes for the cosmic microwave background. His argument is an example of the fallacy of affirming the consequent.

Another mixed hypothetical syllogism has the following form:

1. If p, then q.

2. Not q.

3. Therefore, not p.

This is a valid argument as can be seen by substituting the phrases for the symbols.

1. If it is snowing, then it must be cold outside.

2. It is not cold outside.

3. Therefore, it is not snowing.

Since the second premise denies that the consequent (q) is true, this valid argument is called "denying the consequent" or, in Latin, *modus tollens,* which means the "method of denying."

Denying the antecedent

As before, there is an argument that is superficially similar to *modus tollens,* but is actually a fallacy. It has this form:

1. If p, then q.

2. Not p.

3. Therefore, not q.

We can see that this is fallacious by substituting the phrases for the symbols:

1. If it is snowing, then it must be cold outside.

2. It is not snowing.

3. Therefore, it is not cold outside.

But clearly, it could be cold outside and still not snow. So, the argument is invalid. Since the second premise denies that the antecedent (p) is true, this fallacy is called "denying the antecedent." Here are some examples:

1. If we found dinosaurs and humans next to each other in the same rock formation, then they must have lived at the same time.

2. We do not find them next to each other in the same rock formation.

3. Therefore, they did not live at the same time.

This denies the antecedent and is fallacious. There could be several reasons why dinosaur fossils are not normally found next to human fossils; perhaps dinosaurs and people typically did not live in the same area (as one hypothetical explanation).

1. If God were to perform a miracle in front of me right now, then that would prove He exists.

2. God is not performing a miracle in front of me right now.

3. Therefore, He doesn't exist.

Again, this denies the antecedent. God is under no obligation to perform a miracle at the whim of one of His creations. Nor is it likely that the atheist would accept a given miracle as legitimate anyway—preferring to trust that future studies will reveal that the event is explainable by natural law.

Summary

(1) If p, then q. (2) p. (3) Therefore, q.	valid: *modus ponens*
(1) If p, then q. (2) q. (3) Therefore, p.	fallacy of affirming the consequent
(1) If p, then q. (2) Not q. (3) Therefore, not p.	valid: *modus tollens*
(1) If p, then q. (2) Not p. (3) Therefore, not q.	fallacy of denying the antecedent

Conclusions

It is the obligation of the Christian to be rational—to pattern our thinking after God's (Isaiah 55:7–8). We are to be imitators of Him (Ephesians 5:1) and to think in a way that is consistent with God's logical nature (Romans 12:2).

Not only do we belong to God as his creations, but He has redeemed us by His Son. Our commitment to Christ, therefore, must extend to all aspects of our life. We are to love the Lord with all our heart, soul, strength, and mind (Luke 10:27).

We hope that you have enjoyed this overview of logical fallacies and that the information presented here will help in your defense of the faith. For more information on logical fallacies—including many not covered in this pocket guide—consider reading *The Ultimate Proof of Creation*, which has two chapters on how to spot fallacies, and *Discerning Truth*, which expands on the material in this pocket guide. A good textbook on logic or logical fallacies may also be helpful, even if it is not written from a Christian perspective.[1] Christian apologist Dr. Greg Bahnsen also has a lecture series on logic and critical thinking that may be very helpful; it is available from the Covenant Media Foundation.

---

1. I recommend *Introduction to Logic*—an excellent textbook on logic by Copi and Cohen.
    I also recommend *With Good Reason* by S. Morris Engel, which is a book on informal
    fallacies.

Atheism: An Irrational Worldview

Atheists are "coming out of the closet" and becoming more vocal about their message that "there is no God." Professor Richard Dawkins (Britain's leading atheist) is encouraging those who share his views to express their opinion. Author of *The God Delusion*, Dawkins says he wants to "free children from being indoctrinated with the religion of their parents or their community."[1] Will Christians be prepared to "give an answer" to the atheists' claims?[2]

Materialistic atheism is one of the easiest worldviews to refute. A materialistic atheist believes that nature is all that there is. He believes that there is no transcendent God who oversees and maintains creation. Many atheists believe that their worldview is rational—and scientific. However, by embracing materialism, the atheist has destroyed the possibility of knowledge, as well as science and technology. In other words, if atheism were true, it would be impossible to prove anything!

Here's why:

Reasoning involves using the laws of logic. These include the law of non-contradiction which says that you can't have **A** and **not-A** at the same time and in the same relationship. For example, the statement "My car is in the parking lot, and it is not the case that my car is in the parking lot" is necessarily false by the law of non-contradiction. Any rational person would accept this law. But why is this law true? Why should there be a law of non-contradiction, or for that matter, any laws of reasoning? The Christian can answer this question. For the Christian there is an absolute standard for reasoning; we are to pattern our thoughts after God's. The laws of logic are a reflection of the way God thinks. The law of non-contradiction is not simply one person's opinion of how we ought to think, rather it stems from God's self-consistent nature. God cannot deny Himself (2 Timothy 2:13), and so, the way God upholds the universe will necessarily be non-contradictory.

Laws of logic are God's standard for thinking. Since God is an unchanging, sovereign, immaterial Being, the laws of logic are abstract, universal, invariant entities. In other words, they are not made of matter—they apply everywhere and at all times. Laws of logic are contingent upon God's unchanging nature. And they are necessary for logical reasoning. Thus, rational reasoning would be impossible without the biblical God.

The materialistic atheist can't have laws of logic. He believes that everything that exists is material—part of the physical world. But laws of logic are not physical. You can't stub your toe on a law of logic. Laws of logic cannot exist in the atheist's world, yet he uses them to try to reason. This is inconsistent. He is borrowing from the Christian worldview to argue against the Christian worldview. The atheist's view cannot be rational because he uses things (laws of logic) that cannot exist according to his profession.

The debate over the existence of God is a bit like a debate over the existence of air.[3] Can you imagine someone arguing that air doesn't actually exist? He would offer seemingly excellent "proofs" against the existence of air, while simultaneously breathing air and expecting that we can hear his words as the sound is transmitted through the air. In order for us to hear and understand his claim, it would have to be wrong. Likewise, the atheist, in arguing that God does not exist must use laws of logic that only make sense if God does exist. In order for his argument to make sense, it would have to be wrong.

How can the atheist respond?

The atheist might say, "Well, I can reason just fine, and I don't believe in God." But this is no different than the critic of air saying, "Well, I can breathe just fine, and I don't believe in air." This isn't a rational response. Breathing requires air, not a profession of belief in air. Likewise, logical reasoning requires God, not a profession of belief in Him. Of course the atheist can reason; it's because God has made his mind and given him access to the laws of logic—and that's the point. It's because God exists that reasoning is possible. The atheist can reason, but within his own worldview he cannot account for his ability to reason.

The atheist might respond, "Laws of logic are conventions made up by man." But conventions are (by definition) conventional. That is, we all agree to them and so they work—like driving on the right side of the road. But if laws of logic were conventional, then different cultures could adopt different laws of logic (like driving on the left side of the road). So, in some cultures it might be perfectly fine to contradict yourself. In some societies truth could be self-contradictory. Clearly that wouldn't do. If laws of logic are just conventions, then they are not universal laws. Rational debate would be impossible if laws of logic were conventional, because the two opponents could simply pick different standards for reasoning. Each would be right according to his own arbitrary standard.

The atheist might respond, "Laws of logic are material— they are made of electrochemical connections in the brain." But then the laws of logic are not universal; they would not extend beyond the brain. In other words, we couldn't argue that contradictions cannot occur on Mars, since no one's brain is on Mars. In fact, if the laws of logic are just electrochemical connections in the brain, then they would differ somewhat from person to person because everyone has different connections in their brain.

Sometimes an atheist will attempt to answer with a more pragmatic response: "We use the laws of logic because they work." Unfortunately for him, that isn't the question. We all agree the laws of logic work; they work because they're true. The question is why do they exist in the first place? How can the atheist account for absolute standards of reasoning like the laws of logic? How can non-material things like laws exist if the universe is material only?

As a last resort, the atheist may give up a strictly materialistic view and agree that there are immaterial, universal laws. This is a huge concession; after all, if a person is willing to concede that immaterial, universal, unchanging entities can exist, then he must consider the possibility that God exists. But this concession does not save the atheist's position. He must still justify the laws of logic. Why do they exist? And what is the point of contact between the material physical world and the immaterial world of logic? In other words, why does the material universe feel compelled to obey immaterial laws? The atheist cannot answer these questions. His worldview cannot be justified; it is arbitrary and thus irrational.

Conclusions

Clearly, atheism is not a rational worldview. It is self-refuting because the atheist must first assume the opposite of what he is trying to prove in order to be able to prove anything. As Dr. Cornelius VanTil put it, "[A]theism presupposes theism." Laws of logic require the existence of God—and not just any god, but the Christian God. Only the God of the Bible can be the foundation for knowledge (Proverbs 1:7; Colossians 2:3). Since the God of Scripture is immaterial, sovereign, and beyond time, it makes sense to have laws of logic that are immaterial, universal, and unchanging. Since God has revealed Himself to man, we are able to know and use logic. Since God made the universe and since God made our minds, it makes sense that our minds would have an ability to study and understand the universe. But if the brain is simply the result of mindless evolutionary processes that conveyed some sort of survival value in the past, why should we trust its conclusions? If the universe and our minds are simply the results of time and chance, as the atheist contends, why would we expect that the mind could make sense of the universe? How could science and technology be possible?

Rational thinking, science, and technology make sense in a Christian worldview. The Christian has a basis for these things; the atheist does not. This is not to say that atheists cannot be rational about some things. They can because they too are made in God's image and have access to God's laws of logic. But they have no rational basis for rationality within their own worldview. Likewise, atheists can be moral, but they have no basis for that morality according to what they claim to believe. An atheist is a walking bundle of contradictions. He reasons and does science, yet he denies the very God that makes reasoning and science possible. On the other hand, the Christian worldview is consistent and makes sense of human reasoning and experience.

---

1. "Atheists arise: Dawkins spreads the A-word among America's unbelievers" *The Guardian*, October 1st, 2007. http://www.guardian.co.uk/usa/story/0,,2180901,00.html

2. See 1 Peter 3:15.

3. Christian philosopher Dr. Greg Bahnsen often used this analogy. Dr. Bahnsen was known as the "man atheists most feared."

Natural laws exist because
the Creator who is logical has
imposed order on His universe.

God & Natural Law

The law of biogenesis states that life always comes from life. Both observational science and Genesis 1 tell us that organisms reproduce after their own kind. This and other natural laws exist because the universe has a Creator who is logical and has imposed order on His universe.

The universe obeys certain rules—laws to which all things must adhere. These laws are precise, and many of them are mathematical in nature. Natural laws are hierarchical in nature; secondary laws of nature are based on primary laws of nature, which have to be just right in order for our universe to be possible. But, where did these laws come from, and why do they exist? If the universe were merely the accidental by-product of a big bang, then why should it obey orderly principles—or any principles at all for that matter? Such laws are consistent with biblical creation. Natural laws exist because the universe has a Creator God who is logical and has imposed order on His universe (Genesis 1:1).

The Word of God

Everything in the universe, every plant and animal, every rock, every particle of matter or light wave, is bound by laws which it has no choice but to obey. The Bible tells us that there are laws of nature—"ordinances of heaven and earth" (Jeremiah 33:25). These laws describe the way God normally accomplishes His will in the universe.

God's logic is built into the universe, and so the universe is not haphazard or arbitrary. It obeys laws of chemistry that are logically derived from the laws of physics, many of which can be logically derived from other laws of physics and laws of mathematics. The most fundamental laws of nature exist only because God wills them to; they are the logical, orderly way that the Lord upholds and sustains the universe He has created. The atheist is unable to account for the logical, orderly state of the universe. Why should the universe obey laws if there is no law-giver? But laws of nature are perfectly consistent with biblical creation. In fact, the Bible is the foundation for natural laws.

The law of life (biogenesis)

There is one well-known law of life: the law of biogenesis. This law states simply that life always comes from life. This is what observational science tells us: organisms reproduce other organisms after their own kind. Historically, Louis Pasteur disproved one alleged case of spontaneous generation; he showed that life comes from previous life. Since then, we have seen that this law is universal—with no known exceptions. This is, of course, exactly what we would expect from the Bible. According to Genesis 1, God supernaturally created the first diverse kinds of life on earth and made them to reproduce after their kind. Notice that molecules-to-man evolution violates the law of biogenesis. Evolutionists believe that life (at least once) spontaneously formed from nonliving chemicals. But this is inconsistent with the law of biogenesis. Real science confirms the Bible.

Everything in the universe, every plant and animal, every rock, every particle of matter or light wave, is bound by laws which it has no choice but to obey.

The laws of chemistry

Life requires a specific chemistry. Our bodies are powered by chemical reactions and depend on the laws of chemistry operating in a uniform fashion. Even the information that makes up any living being is stored on a long molecule called DNA. Life as we know it would not be possible if the laws of chemistry were different. God created the laws of chemistry in just the right way so that life would be possible.

The laws of chemistry give different properties to the various elements (each made of one type of atom) and compounds (made up of two or more types of atoms that are bonded together) in the universe. For example, when given sufficient activation energy, the lightest element (hydrogen) will react with oxygen to form water. Water itself has some interesting properties, such as the ability to hold an unusually large amount of heat energy. When frozen, water forms crystals with six-sided symmetry (which is why snowflakes are generally six-sided). Contrast this with salt (sodium chloride) crystals, which tend to form cubes. It is the six-fold symmetry of water ice that causes "holes" in its crystal, making it less dense than its own liquid. That's why ice floats in water (whereas essentially all other frozen compounds sink in their own liquid).

The properties of elements and compounds are not arbitrary. In fact, the elements can be logically organized into a periodic table based on their physical properties. Substances in the same column on the table tend to have similar properties. This follows because elements in a vertical column have the same outer electron structures. These outermost electrons determine the physical characteristics of the atom. The periodic table did not happen by chance. Atoms and molecules have their various properties because their electrons are bound by the laws of quantum physics. In other words, chemistry is based on physics. If the laws of quantum physics were just a bit different, atoms might not even be possible. God designed the laws of physics just right so that the laws of chemistry would come out the way He wanted them to.

The laws of planetary motion

The creation scientist Johannes Kepler discovered that the planets in our solar system obey three laws of nature. He found that planets orbit in ellipses (not perfect circles as had been previously thought) with the sun at one focus of the ellipse; thus a given planet is sometimes closer to the sun than at other times. Kepler also found that planets sweep out equal areas in equal times—in other words, planets speed up as they get closer to the sun within their orbit. And third, Kepler found the exact mathematical relationship between a planet's distance from the sun (a) and its orbital period (p); planets that are farther from the sun take much longer to orbit than planets that are closer (expressed as $p^2=a^3$). Kepler's laws also apply to the orbits of moons around a given planet.[1]

As with the laws of chemistry, these laws of planetary motion are not fundamental. Rather, they are the logical derivation of other laws of nature. In fact, it was another creation scientist (Sir Isaac Newton) who discovered that Kepler's laws could be derived mathematically from certain laws of physics—specifically, the laws of gravity and motion (which Newton himself formulated).

The laws of physics

The field of physics describes the behavior of the universe at its most fundamental level. There are many different laws of physics. They describe the way the universe operates today. Some laws of physics describe how light propagates, how energy is transported, how gravity operates, how mass moves through space, and many other phenomena. The laws of physics are usually mathematical in nature; some laws of physics can be described with a concise formula, such as $E=mc^2$. The simple formula $F=ma$ shows how an object with mass (m) will accelerate (a) when a net force (F) is applied to it. It is amazing that every object in the universe consistently obeys these rules.

There is a hierarchy in physics: some laws of physics can be derived from other laws of physics. For example, Einstein's famous formula $E=mc^2$ can be derived from the principles and equations of special relativity. Conversely, there are many laws of physics that cannot be derived from other laws of physics; many of these are suspected to be derivative principles, but scientists have not yet deduced their derivation.

And some laws of physics may be truly fundamental (not based on other laws); they exist only because God wills them to. In fact, this must be the case for at least one law of physics (and perhaps several)—the most fundamental. (Logically, this is because if the most fundamental law were based on some other law, it would not be the most fundamental law.)

The laws of physics (along with their associated constants) are fine-tuned in just the right way so that life, particularly human life, is possible. This fact is called the "anthropic principle."[1]

[1]*Anthropic* comes from the Greek word for man, *anthropos*.

The laws of mathematics

Notice that the laws of physics are highly mathematical in nature. They would not work if there were not also laws of mathematics. Mathematical laws and principles include the rules of addition, the transitive property, the commutative properties of addition and multiplication, the binomial theorem, and many others. Like the laws of physics, some laws and properties of mathematics can be derived from other mathematical principles. But unlike the laws of physics, the laws of mathematics are abstract; they are not "attached" to any specific part of the universe. It is possible to imagine a universe where the laws of physics are different, but it is difficult to imagine a (consistent) universe where the laws of mathematics are different.[2]

The laws of mathematics are an example of a "transcendent truth." They must be true regardless of what kind of universe God created. This may be because God's nature is logical and mathematical; thus, any universe He chose to create would necessarily be mathematical in nature. The secular naturalist cannot account for the laws of mathematics. Certainly he would believe in mathematics and would use mathematics, but he is unable to account for the existence of mathematics within a naturalistic framework since mathematics is not a part of the physical universe. However, the Christian understands that there is a God beyond the universe and that mathematics reflects the thoughts of the Lord. Understanding math is, in a sense, "thinking God's thoughts after Him"[3] (though in a limited, finite way, of course).

Some have supposed that mathematics is a human invention. It is said that if human history had been different, an entirely different form of math would have been constructed—one with alternate laws, theorems, axioms, etc. But such thinking is not consistent. Are we to believe that the universe did not obey mathematical laws before people discovered them? Did the planets orbit differently before Kepler discovered that $p^2=a^3$? Clearly, mathematical laws are something that human beings have discovered, not invented. The only thing that might have been different (had human history taken a different course) is the notation—the way in which we choose to express mathematical truths through symbols. But these truths exist regardless of how they are expressed. Mathematics could rightly be called the "language of creation."

The laws of logic

All the laws of nature, from physics and chemistry to the law of biogenesis, depend on the laws of logic. Like mathematics, the laws of logic are transcendent truths. We cannot imagine that the laws of logic could be anything different from what they are. Take the law of non-contradiction for example. This law states that you cannot have both "A" and "not A" at the same time and in the same relationship. Without the laws of logic, reasoning would be impossible. But where do the laws of logic come from?

The atheist cannot account for the laws of logic, even though he or she must accept that they exist in order to do any rational thinking. But according to the Bible, God is logical. Indeed, the law of non-contradiction reflects God's nature; God cannot lie (Numbers 23:19) or be tempted with evil (James 1:13) since these things contradict His perfect nature. Since we have been made in God's image, we instinctively know the laws of logic. We are able to reason logically (though because of finite minds and sin we don't always think entirely logically).

The uniformity of nature

The laws of nature are uniform. They do not (arbitrarily) change, and they apply throughout the whole cosmos. The laws of nature apply in the future just as they have applied in the past; this is one of the most basic assumptions in all of science. Without this assumption, science would be impossible. If the laws of nature suddenly and arbitrarily changed tomorrow, then past experimental results would tell us nothing about the future. Why is it that we can depend on the laws of nature to apply consistently throughout time? The secular scientists cannot justify this important assumption. But the Christian can because the Bible gives us the answer. God is Lord over all creation and sustains the universe in a consistent and logical way. God does not change, and so He upholds the universe in a consistent, uniform way throughout time (Jeremiah 33:25).

Conclusion

We have seen that the laws of nature depend on other laws of nature, which ultimately depend on God's will. Thus, God created the laws of physics in just the right way so that the laws of chemistry would be correct, so that life can exist. It is doubtful that any human would have been able to solve such a complex puzzle. Yet, the Lord has done so. The atheist cannot account for these laws of nature (even though he agrees that they must exist), for such laws are inconsistent with naturalism. Yet, they are perfectly consistent with the Bible. We expect the universe to be organized in a logical, orderly fashion and to obey uniform laws because the universe was created by the power of God.

---

1. However, the constant of proportionality is different for the third law. This is due to the fact that the sun has a different mass than the planets.

2. Granted, there are different systems of starting definitions and axioms that allow for some variation in mathematical systems of thought (alternate geometries, etc.). But most of the basic principles remain unchanged.

3. This phrase is attributed to the creation astronomer Johannes Kepler.

Eve attempted to use her own reason in opposition to God's Word.

Faith vs. Reason

Some Christians have the idea that faith and reason are in conflict, divided by some unbridgeable chasm. They think that one takes over where the other leaves off. In reality, faith and reason work together seamlessly to help us know and love our Maker.

Many Christians perceive a conflict between reason and faith. On the one hand, God tells us to reason (Isaiah 1:18). We are to have a good reason for what we believe, and we are to be always ready to share that reason with other people (1 Peter 3:15). So we attempt to show unbelievers that our belief in the Scriptures is reasonable, justified, and logically defensible. The Bible makes sense.

On the other hand, we are supposed to have faith. We are supposed to trust God and not lean on our own understanding (Proverbs 3:5). The Bible tells us that the "just shall live by faith" (Romans 1:17;Galatians 3:11). It seems that we are supposed to trust God regardless of whether His words make sense to our understanding.

So, which is it? Are we to live by reason or by faith? Are we supposed to rely upon our intellect, drawing rational conclusions, rejecting those things that don't make sense? Or are we to accept the teachings of Scripture without regard to logic and reason, even if it does not make any sense?

The apparent conflict between faith and reason troubles many people. When they are properly understood in their biblical context, however, any apparent conflict disappears.

This apparent conflict troubles many people. But it stems from a critical misconception about the meaning of both faith and reason. When both terms are properly defined in their biblical context, any apparent conflict disappears. Yes, we are to have good reasons for what we believe, and we are also to have faith. In fact, without the latter, we could not have the former.

Misconceptions of faith

Mark Twain once defined faith as "believing what you know ain't so."[1] Perhaps this is what many people have in mind when they think of the word *faith*. Indeed some people seem to pride themselves in their belief in the irrational—thinking that such "faith" is very pious. "Why do I believe in the Bible? Well, I guess I just have faith."

But is this what the Bible means when it uses the word faith? Not at all. The Bible does not promote a belief in the irrational or any type of unwarranted "blind faith."

Some people have said, "Faith takes over where reason leaves off." Taken this way, rationality is seen as a bridge that reaches only partway across a great chasm; faith is needed to complete the bridge and reach the other side.

People who take this view would say that Christianity cannot be proven, that reason leads us most of the way to God and then we must make a "leap of faith" in order to say that Jesus is Lord. This is a very common view among Christians. But this is not what God's Word teaches about faith.

Biblical faith

The Bible itself tells us what faith is. Hebrews 11:1 tells us that faith is the substance of things hoped for, the evidence of things not seen. So biblical faith is not blind but is strongly warranted confidence. The phrase "hoped for" does not imply a mere wishful thinking as in "I sure hope the weather is nice next week." Rather, the Greek word ($ελπιζω$) indicates a confident expectation: the kind of confidence we have when we have a good reason to believe something.

Biblically, faith is having confidence in something you have not experienced with your senses. Biblical faith is not "blind"; it's not the act of "believing without a reason." Just the opposite; biblical faith is the act of believing in something unseen for which we do have a good reason.

For example, when we believe that God will keep a promise, this constitutes faith because we cannot "see" it and yet we have a good reason for it: God has demonstrated that He keeps His promises.

The place of reason

As many people have misunderstandings of faith, they also have misunderstandings of reason. Reason is a tool that God has given us that allows us to draw conclusions and inferences from other information, such as the information He has given us in His Word. Reason is an essential part of Christianity; God tells us to reason (Isaiah 1:18) as the apostle Paul did (Acts 17:17).

In fact, I could not know that I am saved apart from using reason. After all, the Bible nowhere says that "Dr. Lisle is saved." Instead it tells me that "if you confess with your mouth the Lord Jesus and believe in your heart that God has raised Him from the dead, you will be saved" (Romans 10:9). I have genuinely acknowledged that Jesus is Lord, and I believe that God raised Him from the dead. Therefore, I am saved. I must use logical reasoning to draw this conclusion.[2]

This is perfectly appropriate and is the kind of reasoning God expects us to use. We are to reason from the principles of God's Word.[3]

People misuse reason when they frame their worldview apart from God's Word. This can involve either treating reason as its own ultimate standard (in other words, a replacement for God's Word) or tossing it aside as irrelevant to faith.

Neither of these positions is biblical. We are never to attempt to reason in opposition to the Word of God. That is to say we are not to treat God's Word as a mere hypothesis that is subject to our fallible understanding of the universe.

This, after all, was Eve's mistake. She attempted to use her mind and senses to judge God's Word (Genesis 3:6). This was sinful and irrational; she was trying to use a fallible standard to judge an infallible one.

We are never to "reason" in such an absurd, sinful way. Instead, we are supposed to reason from God's Word, taking it as our ultimate unquestionable starting point. Any alternative is arbitrary and self-refuting.[4] Reason is not a substitute for God; rather, it is a gift from God.

On the other hand, we are not to reject reason. God is rational,[5] and so we should be, too (Ephesians 5:1). We are commanded to seek wisdom and understanding (Proverbs 4:5, 7). God wants us to use the mind He has given us. But He wants us to use our minds properly, in a way that is honoring to Him.

Faith is necessary for reason

Biblical faith and biblical reasoning actually work very well together. In fact, faith is a prerequisite for reason. In order to reason about anything we must have faith that there are laws of logic which correctly prescribe the correct chain of reasoning. Since laws of logic cannot be observed with the senses, our confidence in them is a type of faith.

For the Christian, it is a reasonable, justified faith. The Christian would expect to find a standard of reasoning that reflects the thinking of the biblical God; that's what laws of logic are.[6] On the other hand, the unbeliever cannot account for laws of logic with his or her own worldview.[7]

Since laws of logic are necessary for reasoning, and since the Christian faith is the only faith system that can make sense of them,[8] it follows that the Christian faith is the logical foundation for all reasoning (Proverbs 1:7; Colossians 2:3). This isn't to say, of course, that non-Christians cannot reason. Rather, it simply means they are being inconsistent when they reason; they are borrowing from a worldview contrary to the one they profess.

Since reason would be impossible without laws of logic, which stem from the Christian faith, we have a very good reason for our faith: without our faith we could not reason. Even unbelievers (inconsistently) rely upon Christian principles, such as logic, whenever they reason about anything. So the Christian has a good reason for his or her faith. In fact, the Christian faith system makes reason possible.

Can we "reason" someone to heaven?

Although reasoning from the Scriptures is an important part of the Christian's life, reason alone is not sufficient to lead us to Christ.

After the fall of Adam, human beings no longer possessed the ability to correctly understand spiritual matters (1 Corinthians 2:14). It is our nature to distort the truth (2 Peter 3:16). So we

need the help of the Holy Spirit even to understand and accept the fact that Jesus is Lord (1 Corinthians 12:3).

This explains why it is impossible to "reason someone into heaven." Salvation is accomplished by God's grace received through faith in Christ alone (Ephesians 2:8; Romans 3:24; Titus 3:5). It is ultimately the Holy Spirit who convinces people and enables them to receive Christ (John 16:8–15).

Some may ask, "Why then should we do apologetics? Why should we try to reason with people if it is the Holy Spirit who will ultimately convince them?"

There are two reasons.

First, God tells us to. We are to be ready at all times to give a good reason for our faith (1 Peter 3:15). So it is our duty as followers of Christ to preach the gospel (2 Timothy 4:2) and reason with unbelievers (Acts 17:17).

Second, God can bless our discussions with unbelievers and use them as part of the process by which He brings people to Himself (Romans 10:13–14). Although salvation is accomplished by Christ alone, God has given us the privilege of telling others about this good news and making a reasoned defense of it.

Reasoning is a crucial part of defending the faith. But we must always keep in mind that conversion is up to God alone. It is not our job to "convince" the unbeliever—nor can we. It is our job to make a good case; it is the Holy Spirit's prerogative alone to bring repentance.

One Christian may plant a seed, and another water it, but God alone brings the increase (1 Corinthians 3:6–7).

1. Mark Twain, *Following the Equator: A Journey around the World*, chapter 12.

2. I recognize that not all who say with their lips that Christ is Lord are genuinely saved (Matthew 7:21–23). Not all faith is saving faith (James 2:19–20). The point here is that I could never know that I am saved without using logic to reason from the Scriptures.

3. Even the atheist must use the principles found in God's Word to reason properly (though of course he or she would not admit it). He or she must use laws of logic (which stem from God's nature) and induction (which relies on God's consistent sustaining power) in order to think properly about anything.

4. See the author's book *The Ultimate Proof of Creation*, chapter 9.

5. God does not violate the laws of logic. This is necessarily so because laws of logic are "reflections" of the way God thinks. Since God is always true to Himself and never denies Himself (2 Timothy 2:13), and since all truth and knowledge are in Him (Colossians 2:3; John 14:6), all truth will have an internal consistency that we describe as the laws of logic.

6. The law of noncontradiction, for example, is an expression of the self-consistent nature of God. We should not conclude from this that we can think exactly as God thinks; after all, He is infinite and we are finite, He is beyond time, and we must think within time. Nonetheless, we are able to line up our thinking (in a limited way) with God's nature. We too can be consistent and rational, though because of sin we don't always do this.

7. See *The Ultimate Proof of Creation*, chapter 3.

8. Laws of logic are universal, invariant, abstract, exceptionless entities. Only the Christian worldview can make sense of these properties, because only the Christian worldview has a God who is fully self-consistent, omnipresent, and beyond time, who has made us in His image and who has revealed some of His thoughts to us objectively in His written Word. So, we can have confidence in the laws of logic and their properties. This position is demonstrated more rigorously in *The Ultimate Proof of Creation*, chapter 3.

Author Biography

Dr. Jason Lisle graduated *summa cum laude* from Ohio Wesleyan University, where he double-majored in physics and astronomy and minored in mathematics. He did graduate work at the University of Colorado where he earned a master's degree and a PhD in astrophysics.

While there, Dr. Lisle used the SOHO spacecraft to investigate motions on the surface of the sun as well as solar magnetism and subsurface weather. His thesis was entitled "Probing the Dynamics of Solar Supergranulation and its Interaction with Magnetism."

Among other things, Dr. Lisle discovered a previously unknown polar alignment of supergranules (solar convection cells) and discovered evidence of solar giant cells. He has also authored a number of papers in both secular and creation literature.

Dr. Lisle was a researcher, speaker, and writer for Answers in Genesis from 2004 to 2011. He designed several planetarium programs for the Stargazer's Room at the Creation Museum in Northern Kentucky (near Cincinnati, Ohio). Among these programs is the very popular Created Cosmos—an examination of the amazing size of God's universe.

Dr. Lisle has authored a number of books and articles. His books include Taking Back Astronomy, The Ultimate Proof of Creation, Discerning Truth, and Old-Earth Creationism on Trial, co-authored with Tim Chaffey. He is also a contributing author for The New Answers Books volumes 1 and 2.

Dr. Lisle is currently the Director of Research at the Institute for Creation Research.

Looking for Truth

Many people have abandoned the idea that there is any way to know the truth about many topics. This applies to many areas of life, but people seem to realize that this type of relativism doesn't work when it comes to their bank accounts or putting gas in their car. There is a disconnect between what people want reality to be and what it actually is.

Many people have rejected the idea that it is possible to know whether or not there is a God. They claim religious and spiritual matters are merely subjective, but they offer no proof for these claims. Some suggest that all roads lead to heaven or that everyone gets to determine what happens to them when they die. Neither of these options is logically possible. If all roads lead to heaven, then all of the claims of the various religions must be true.

Examining the claims of various religions shows that they contradict one another. Muslims believe that there is only one god, Allah, that he is distant, and that he has revealed himself through the writings in the Koran. Buddhists do not believe there is a god, and Hindus adopt new gods at every turn. Rastafarians believe they can only connect with the divine through drug-induced states and that Jesus returned as Haile Selassie. Christians believe God exists as the Trinity and that Jesus has not yet returned to the earth.

Because these various religions make claims that are contradictory, they cannot all be true. Either Christians are correct and Jesus is still to return or the Rastafarians are correct and Jesus was present as an Ethiopian Emperor. Simple logic tells us that both cannot be true. But this leads us to ask another important question—where did logic come from?

The Bible presents the only possible answer to this question and the conditions of the reality we live in. That might sound like an outrageous claim, but if the Bible is not true, then we have no logically coherent explanation for the universe we live in. All other systems of thinking are based on some sort of logical fallacy. The Bible alone reveals the nature and character of the God who created the entire universe and has done so in a logical way. He has created a universe that operates according to orderly principles where logic can be used to understand the world around us.

If the universe were simply the result of chance processes, why would we expect the order we see? Only a universe created by an all-knowing, all-powerful Creator could exhibit the qualities we see in our universe. Since God is the Creator, He has right to rule over His creation. He has established laws for his creatures to follow and He has communicated those to us in the Bible.

When God originally created the universe, He described everything as "very good." He created an orderly universe that was functioning in perfect harmony. Then, part of His creation rebelled against the Creator. Adam and Eve disobeyed God and plunged the entire universe into a corrupted state. Since we are all descendants of Adam and Eve, we bear the scars of that corruption—we have sinned against God just like Adam.

If you doubt this, just stop and examine your heart. God demands perfect obedience from His creatures. If you are honest with yourself, you will recognize that you are not perfect. You might object that no one is perfect and that would mean that everyone is subject to God's judgment. Actually, that is the awful truth of humanity. All have sinned and fall short of the glory of God (Romans 3:23). If you are not perfect in moral character (you have lied, lusted, put yourself before others, ignored God, or given your affections to money and happiness over God), God's wrath against sin is set against you.

The Bible describes God as a just Judge who will judge everyone according to their deeds. Psalm 7:11–17 describe the state of man before God:

> God is a just judge, and God is angry with the wicked every day. If he does not turn back, He will sharpen His sword; He bends His bow and makes it ready. He also prepares for Himself instruments of death; He makes His arrows into fiery shafts. Behold, the wicked brings forth iniquity; yes, he conceives trouble and brings forth falsehood. He made a pit and dug it out, and has fallen into the ditch which he made. His trouble shall return upon his own head, and his violent dealing shall come down on his own crown. I will praise the Lord according to His righteousness, and will sing praise to the name of the Lord Most High.

That sounds like bad news—God is intent on judging the wicked acts of mankind. Because He is just, He must punish sin. But the Bible also reveals the mercy of God in many places. He shows that mercy in providing a substitute to take the punishment that every human deserves for their sin.

God the Son, Jesus Christ, stepped into this corrupted world as a baby in a manger. He lived a life of moral perfection on this earth and then willingly offered His life as a ransom for many by dying on the Cross (Mark 10:45). As He hung on the Cross, God the Father poured out His wrath against sin upon the perfect Son. Jesus bore the penalty for sin in order that He could take the place of sinful mankind and turn away the wrath of God.

The Bible says that God's wrath against sin is satisfied in Jesus's work on the Cross for all of those who repent of their sin and place their trust in Christ. This means turning away from the idea that we can do enough good to merit God's favor, and trusting that only the finished work of Christ can save us from God's wrath. God's mercy and grace are demonstrated in this great exchange: Jesus takes the punishment for our sin and gives us His righteous record.

When you stand before God on the Day of Judgment and He asks you why you should be allowed to enter into His kingdom, how will you respond? Will you tell Him He is an ogre to expect mankind to obey His commands? Will you tell Him of all of the "good things" you have done to earn entrance? Or, will you tell Him that you have no right of your own to enter into His kingdom, but that what His Son has done on your behalf is the only reason you should be allowed in? When you cry out to God for mercy for your sins and surrender your life to Christ, He will clothe you with His robes of righteousness and you can be welcomed into His kingdom at His expense.

No other religion offers complete forgiveness for sin. Many try to cover it up; many try to pile up good works that might outweigh the bad; many try to ignore the idea and say that there is no sin. Only one of these ideas can be the correct way to deal with sin. Trust that the Creator God of the universe has plainly revealed His plan of salvation in the words of the Bible, and run to Christ for true salvation.